The Just Shall Live by Faith:

Lessons from the Book of Romans

Author – Eld Joel Latimore Jr.

The Just Shall Live by Faith: Lessons from the Book of Romans

Written by Eld Joel Latimore Jr.

© 2025 Eld Joel Latimore Jr.

Latimore Publishing

ISBN (paperback): 979-8-218-82766-3

Scripture quotations are taken from the King James Version (KJV) of the Bible, unless otherwise noted.

Table of Contents

- Dedication

- Preface

- Introduction   **Pg 1**

Chapter 1 – Faith in the Midst…   **Pg 8**

Chapter 2 – The World's Desperate… **Pg 26**

Chapter 3 – Abraham…   **Pg 40**

Chapter 4 – The Stillness Before…   **Pg 54**

Chapter 5 – Faith Under Pressure   **Pg 73**

Chapter 6 – The Storm Arrives   **Pg 86**

Chapter 7 – Life in the Spirit   **Pg 103**

Chapter 8 – More Than Conquerors   **Pg 120**

Chapter 9 – God's Sovereign Mercy   **Pg 140**

Chapter 10 – Living Sacrifices   **Pg 148**

Chapter 11 – Subjection, Love, and…   **Pg 161**

Chapter 12 – Liberty, Responsibility…   **Pg 178**

Chapter 13 – Unity, Endurance, and... **Pg 189**

Chapter 14 – Finishing Well... **Pg 201**

- Epilogue – The Just Shall ... **Pg 210**

- Final Reflection **Pg 214**

- Closing Exhortation **Pg 215**

- Final Prayer **Pg 216**

- About the Author **Pg 217**

- Back Cover Blurb **Pg 219**

Dedication

To every believer who dares to take God at His Word, and to live by faith and not by sight. *"The just shall live by faith."* — **Romans 1:17**

And to my family, mentors, and readers— your prayers, love, and encouragement have helped me to walk this journey step by step.

And to the many fellow Christians who exemplified and modeled for me what a true Christian life looks like.

— Eld Joel Latimore Jr.

Preface

This is not just a book. It is a journey through one of the most powerful letters ever written— the book of Romans.

What you hold in your hands is not theory, but truth that has been tested in the furnace of life.

Romans is more than Paul's masterpiece of theology; it is the Spirit's blueprint for how to live. Its words are not cold doctrine, but living fire—breathed by God, fought for by the saints, prayed over by generations, and still able to transform lives today.

This book is not meant to be a scholarly commentary on Romans, but a Spirit-led journey through its pages. As Paul declared, *"The just shall live by faith."*

In these chapters, we will walk with Paul, listen to his teachings, and see how his words continue to shape our lives today.

Consider this a pastoral commentary—not line by line, but truth by truth, lived out in testimony and applied by faith. I did not write this to impress you. I wrote it because Romans has carried me, corrected me, and reshaped me.

From my days in the military to my years in ministry, from personal failure to the redeeming fire of the Holy Ghost—again and again, I found myself brought back to Romans.

Here I discovered grace when I was guilty, hope when I was hopeless, and strength when I was weak.

Romans is not just a letter—it is a lifeline. It teaches us that **all have sinned**, but also that all may be justified freely by grace.

It shows us that the just shall live by faith, that there is now no condemnation to those who are in Christ, and that nothing shall separate us from the love of God. It walks us from sin to salvation, from flesh to Spirit, from death to life.

If you've ever doubted your salvation, wrestled with sin, or longed to understand God's plan for your life—Romans speaks to you.

If you've ever wondered how to live in the Spirit in a world that pulls you toward the flesh— Romans speaks to you.

If you've ever asked whether God still has a purpose for you, even after your failures— Romans speaks to you.

This book is for *the broken, the called, the forgotten, the overlooked, the misunderstood, the tired, the tempted, and the tenacious.* It is for anyone who dares to believe that God's Word is still alive and that His Spirit still leads His people.

And now, as **Romans 10:17** declares: *"So then faith cometh by hearing, and hearing by the word of God."*

Let the journey begin. The Spirit of God is still speaking through Romans—will you hear Him?

— Eld Joel Latimore Jr.

Introduction

Faith is not a sprint we conquer in one leap; it is a walk we learn, step by step, with God. The book of Romans is God's handbook for that walk.

From the opening chapters that expose our need for salvation, to the Spirit-filled life of **chapter 8,** to the call for transformed living in **chapter 12—** Romans unfolds the Christian life from beginning to end.

This book is not written as an academic commentary, filled with technical notes and theological debates. Others have done that work.

Instead, what you will find here is a Spirit-led guide, written for the everyday believer who desires to live by faith.

My goal is not to impress you with scholarship, but to encourage you with truth—truth that has been lived, tested, and proven in fire.

Romans is often called the "Mount Everest" of Paul's letters, but it is also rightly considered the Christian's Constitution.

Just as a constitution defines the rights and responsibilities of a people, Romans establishes the foundation of what it means to be in Christ.

It is also regarded as Paul's great *Treatise* of the Gospel—his most comprehensive and Spirit-inspired explanation of *salvation, justification, sanctification, and glorification.*

Here we find the charter of grace, the bill of rights for the redeemed, and the Spirit's framework for a life of *holiness, freedom, and faith.*

In these pages, we will not go line by line through every verse, but we will draw out the heartbeat of Romans—**the call to live by faith.**

We will walk with Abraham as he believed against hope, listen to Paul as he proclaims *"no condemnation"* in Christ, and hear the Spirit's assurance that nothing can separate us from the love of God.

We will take the great doctrines of Romans out of the clouds and into the soil of daily living, where faith must be practiced. This journey is not for the curious alone—**it is for the committed.**

- If you are weary of empty religion and hungry for living faith, Romans is your guide.

- If you have stumbled in sin and wondered whether God still has a plan for you, Romans will restore your hope.

- If you long to know the power of the Spirit and the freedom of grace, Romans will lead you there.

So, open your heart as you open these pages. The just shall live by faith. And through Romans—the Christian's Constitution and Paul's Treatise of the Gospel—we will learn together what that truly means.

A Reader's Question:

"What does it mean when the Scripture says, *'The just shall live by faith'?*"

Answer:

The phrase, found in **Romans 1:17, Habakkuk 2:4, Galatians 3:11,** and **Hebrews 10:38**, declares the foundation of the Christian life. The *"just"* are those justified by God through faith in Jesus Christ, not by works or human merit.

To *"live"* means more than existing—it is to walk daily in relationship with God, guided by His Spirit and sustained by His promises.

"By faith" points us to active trust, leaning on God's Word even when circumstances seem impossible. Abraham models this truth when he believed God, and it was counted to him for righteousness.

This truth shapes everything that follows in Romans: *salvation, sanctification, and victory all flow not from human effort but from faith in Christ.* To live by faith is to live as a new creation, free to glorify God with our whole life.

Romans not only defines our faith but demonstrates that the gospel is practical. If we live biblically, according to the New Testament teachings and not man-made doctrine, I promise you, it will work—if you work it. **I am a witness.**

— Eld Joel Latimore Jr.

Chapter 1 – Faith in the Midst of Brokenness

In the heart of the city, the nights are long and the mornings offer no relief.

A young man sits on the cracked steps of a run-down apartment building, head in his hands. He has tried to escape the cycle—*drugs, jail, false promises*—but each time he ends up back where he started. He feels the weight of failure pressing down on him, and the whispers in his mind tell him that he is nothing, that life will never change.

Across the street, a woman stands in line at the corner store, her two children tugging at her sleeve. Her paycheck is already gone, swallowed by overdue bills. She wonders if there will ever be enough, if her children will ever know more than the struggle of survival.

At night, when the lights are off, she cries quietly into her pillow, asking if God sees her, if He hears her prayers.

And yet, in the midst of all this brokenness, just a few blocks away, there stands a small church.

The paint may be peeling, the roof may leak, and the congregation may be few, but inside its walls is a treasure that cannot be bought. For within that sanctuary lies the very answer to the pain of the urban community—the gospel of Jesus Christ.

It is here that the weary can find *rest*. Here that the guilty can discover *grace*. Here that the hopeless *can hear a Word that breathes life into dead situations*.

What the world dismisses as a storefront or a forgotten building, heaven sees as a lighthouse in the storm. It was into a world no less broken than ours that the apostle Paul wrote his letter to the Romans.

Rome was the capital of empire—full of power, wealth, and culture—but also saturated with corruption, injustice, and idolatry.

And yet, in the middle of it all, God planted a church. Just as that small storefront church in an urban community carries the answer for broken neighborhoods today, the church in Rome carried the answer for a broken world in Paul's day.

And so, Paul begins his letter this way:

"Paul, a servant of Jesus Christ, called to be an apostle, separated unto the gospel of God,

(Which he had promised afore by his prophets in the holy scriptures,)

Concerning his Son Jesus Christ our Lord, which was made of the seed of David according to the flesh;

And declared to be the Son of God with power, according to the spirit of holiness, by the resurrection from the dead:

By whom we have received grace and apostleship, for obedience to the faith among all nations, for his name:

Among whom are ye also the called of Jesus Christ:

To all that be in Rome, beloved of God, called to be saints: Grace to you and peace from God our Father, and the Lord Jesus Christ." **(Romans 1:1–7)**

From the very start, Paul introduces himself not as a celebrity or a philosopher but as a servant— a man who himself had experienced the saving grace of Jesus Christ.

Once a persecutor of the church, he now stood as a preacher of the very gospel he once tried to destroy. Transformed by grace, he was willing to share that same grace with the believers in Rome.

His authority did not come from Rome's empire, nor from human recognition, accolades, or achievements.

His authority came from the call of God. Paul understood that his mission was not self-promotion, not the pursuit of power, and not the gaining of wealth, but to proclaim Christ crucified and risen—the power of God unto salvation for all who believe.

And his message stretched far beyond Rome's high walls and wealthy palaces. It was not reserved for the educated or the elite. It reached *the forgotten, the slaves, the poor, and the oppressed.*

Paul was clear: the gospel is for all nations, all people, every man and woman, every background, and every condition.

Then Paul declares the truth that would echo through the centuries:

"For I am not ashamed of the gospel of Christ: for it is the power of God unto salvation to every one that believeth; to the Jew first, and also to the Greek. For therein is the righteousness of God revealed from faith to faith: as it is written, The just shall live by faith." **(Romans 1:16–17)**

Some churches talk about power, but the kind of power they preach is often limited—confined to emotional excitement, material gain, or temporary relief.

But when Paul speaks of the power of God, he is not describing a power with boundaries or conditions. He is describing unlimited power, a power that saves, heals, delivers, and transforms.

14

This is not power that runs out when the music stops or when the service ends. It is power that continues working in the believer's life, breaking chains, renewing minds, and reshaping destinies.

What good would salvation be if it only promised heaven but left you bound in the same sins, struggles, and cycles on earth?

The **gospel** is not just about changing your eternal address—it's about changing your life right now.

It has the power *to lift a man out of addiction, to restore dignity to a broken woman, to reconcile families, to reorder priorities, and to breathe hope into communities.*

This is why Paul boldly declared, *"It is the power of God unto salvation."* Salvation is not weak. It is not partial. It is the total work of God, redeeming the whole person—spirit, soul, and body.

But here is the truth: the gospel works if you work it. The Word will only change the areas of your life that you are willing to surrender.

Too many people sit in church Sunday after Sunday hearing about power but never allowing that power to transform them. They hear sermons but go home unchanged because they will not yield their will, their habits, or their desires to God.

Real transformation comes when you stop resisting God and start submitting to Him fully.

When you surrender your whole *spirit, soul, and body* to the Lord, great things begin to happen.

Old habits lose their grip. New desires are birthed. The peace of God replaces the torment of sin. The joy of the Lord floods the heart where despair once lived. The gospel is not a partial fix; it is a total transformation.

Paul could declare unashamedly that the gospel is the power of God because he experienced it himself. The same man who once persecuted the church became its greatest preacher. The same voice that once breathed threats of murder against believers now proclaimed the message of grace.

That is the unlimited power of God—it does not just forgive, it transforms.

Remember, Jesus never said, "I give riches to the poor." What He said was, *"And the poor have the gospel preached to them"* **(Matthew 11:5; Luke 7:22).**

Why? Because the gospel is greater than gold. Riches can run out, but the Word of God endures forever. Wealth may change your bank account, but the gospel changes your life, your heart, and your eternity.

The power of the gospel is not measured in material possessions but in transformed lives.

What good would it be to give a man money *if his soul is still lost, his habits still destructive, and his hope still broken?*

Money might feed him for a day, but the gospel feeds him for a lifetime. Money might change his circumstances temporarily, but the gospel changes his destiny eternally.

That is why Paul called it *"the power of God unto salvation."*

It is not a limited promise of financial blessing, but an unlimited work of grace that *saves, heals, delivers, restores, and up lifts the whole person.*

When the poor receive the gospel, they receive something far richer than silver or gold—*they receive hope, identity, forgiveness, and the promise of eternal life.*

And yet, this gospel is practical: when truly lived out, it teaches *stewardship, honesty, diligence, and discipline*—principles that lift a person out of cycles of poverty and into new life.

The gospel works if you work it. Jesus did not come to hand out money—He came to hand out life, and life more abundantly.

When you surrender your whole *spirit, soul, and body* to the Lord, that life begins to overflow, and even the conditions around you start to shift.

Reflective Questions:

1. In what ways do you see brokenness in your own community that reminds you of the struggles in Rome's world?

2. Paul introduced himself as a servant first. How does this challenge our ideas of leadership, recognition, and success in today's church?

3. Romans 1:16 declares the gospel as "the power of God unto salvation." How have you personally experienced that power?

4. What does it mean for you, right now, to live by faith and not by sight?

5. Who in your family, neighborhood, or circle of influence needs to hear that the gospel is for them — no matter their background?

Reflective Summary:

Paul's message to the Romans is just as urgent for our urban communities today. In a world that praises status, wealth, and power, Paul stripped it all away and called himself first a servant of Jesus Christ.

His authority was not rooted in empire or applause but in the call of God. And his gospel was not reserved for the elite but for every man, woman, and child — including those the world tries to forget.

The gospel is not a ritual, a philosophy, or a cultural badge. It is the power of God unto salvation.

The same gospel that reached *Rome's poor, slaves, and outcasts* is still reaching into neighborhoods where hope feels scarce. And the same truth still holds: **the just shall live by faith.**

Prayer:

Heavenly Father,

We thank You for the gospel that brings life where there is death, hope where there is despair, and strength where there is weakness.

Remind us that our identity is not in wealth, power, or applause, but in being servants of Christ. Teach us to live unashamed of the gospel, confident that it is Your power to save.

Help us shine as lights in our urban communities, bringing hope to the downcast and faith to the forgotten.

In Jesus' name, Amen.

Chapter 2 – The World's Desperate Need for the Gospel

Before Paul begins to teach us how to live by faith, he first takes us through the dark reality of life without God.

From **Romans 1:18 through 3:23**, Paul paints a sobering picture of sin's grip on humanity. He does not sugarcoat it. He does not excuse it. He shows us the desperate condition of the sinner and the universal truth that without Christ, we are all guilty.

This is where the gospel begins—not with comfort, but with conviction. The good news is only good because the bad news is so devastating.

And the bad news is this: sin has corrupted every man, every woman, every family, every nation. No one escapes its reach. Paul declares plainly in **Romans 3:23,** *"For all have sinned, and come short of the glory of God."*

The Gentile World – Sin Without Restraint (Romans 1:18–32)

Paul begins by describing the Gentile world, a world that had rejected God's truth and embraced idolatry.

He writes that God's wrath is revealed against all ungodliness, because although people knew of God through creation, they refused to glorify Him as God.

Instead, they exchanged His truth for lies and worshiped created things rather than the Creator.

This rejection led to *corruption.* Paul describes people being *"given over"* to the lusts of their hearts—*sexual impurity, unnatural desires, greed, envy, deceit, violence, pride, disobedience, and every kind of wickedness.*

When I read these verses, I don't see distant history—I see my own past. I know what it is to be trapped in lust, to believe the lies of the enemy, to chase after things that promised fulfillment but only left me empty.

Sin doesn't announce itself as destruction; it comes dressed as *pleasure, strength, or identity.* But once it gets a grip, it drags you deeper into shame.

I can remember times when I thought I had everything under control. But sin was controlling me. Just like Paul wrote, I *"knew God"* in my head but denied Him in my actions. I exchanged the truth for lies and the peace of God for the torment of guilt.

The Religious World – Sin Behind Religion (Romans 2)

Paul then turns to the Jews, who prided themselves in having the Law of Moses. They judged the Gentiles, but Paul reminds them that outward religion cannot cover inward sin.

He writes, *"For not the hearers of the law are just before God, but the doers of the law shall be justified"* **(Romans 2:13).**

This hits home for many of us who grew up around church. We knew the songs, the Scriptures, and the traditions, but our hearts were far from God.

That was me. I could sit in a service, clap my hands, and still walk out chasing sin. I knew how to look religious, but inside I was *broken, deceived, and enslaved to sin.*

Religion without transformation is deadly because it convinces you that you're fine when in reality you are far from God.

I learned the hard way that knowing about God is not the same as knowing God.

All the World – Sin is Universal (Romans 3:9–23)

Finally, Paul draws the conclusion: both Jew and Gentile, religious and irreligious, rich and poor—all are under sin.

He writes:

"There is none righteous, no, not one:

There is none that understandeth, there is none that seeketh after God.

They are all gone out of the way, they are together become unprofitable;

there is none that doeth good, no, not one."

(Romans 3:10–12)

And then in **verse 23**, he summarizes: *"For all have sinned, and come short of the glory of God."*

This is where the ground is leveled. The addict in the alley and the Pharisee in the temple stand on the same guilty ground before God. The broken in the streets and the proud in the pulpit all share the same desperate need for the gospel.

I was no different. My sins may not have always looked like someone else's, but they carried the same weight of guilt and the same sentence of death. Without Christ, I was lost. Without His grace, I was condemned.

The Gospel is Our Only Hope

Sin is not a bad habit we can break. It is a power that enslaves. It is not a weakness we can grow out of. It is a death sentence that only Jesus can remove. That is why the gospel is desperately needed.

Paul wanted the Romans to understand this before he spoke of *justification, grace, or living by faith.* Because until you realize your need, you won't reach for the remedy.

I had to come face-to-face with my own sin before I could truly appreciate salvation. I had to admit that I was broken before I could be made whole. I had to confess that I was guilty before I could receive mercy.

And so must we all.

Reflective Questions:

1. Why must we first face the reality of sin before we can truly appreciate the gift of salvation?

2. How do you see Paul's description of sin in **Romans 1–3** reflected in our world today?

3. In what ways has sin personally touched your own life, and how has the gospel offered hope and transformation?

4. Why is outward religion without inward change so dangerous?

5. What step can you take today to shift your focus from your problems to the preached Word of God, like the weary man and struggling mother in the illustration?

Reflective Summary:

Paul's words in **Romans 1:18–3:23** bring us face-to-face with a truth we would rather avoid: sin is universal, destructive, and deadly.

From the Gentiles who rejected God outright, to the Jews who hid behind religion, to the final declaration that *"all have sinned"*—Paul levels the ground at the foot of the cross.

None are righteous; none can save themselves. And yet, this sobering truth prepares us for the beauty of the gospel.

The illustration of the weary man and struggling mother reminds us that while sin presses down with despair, the gospel lifts up with hope.

Turning from sin to the Savior is not easy, but it is right. The gospel is not theory—*it is power.* And when believed, it transforms lives, families, and communities.

Prayer for Forgiveness:

Heavenly Father,

I thank You for the truth of Your Word that reveals both my sin and Your salvation. I confess that I have fallen short, and I ask for Your forgiveness.

Lord, help me not to hide behind religion, excuses, or pride, but to turn fully to Christ. Let the power of the gospel transform my spirit, soul, and body.

Give me the courage to surrender every part of my life so that I may walk in Your freedom and truth. May my life bear witness that the just shall live by faith.

In Jesus' name, Amen.

Chapter 3 – Abraham: The Pattern of Saving Faith

As Paul continues in his letter to the Romans, he does not leave us in despair after showing that all have sinned. Instead, he points us to hope, and he chooses Abraham to show us what saving faith looks like.

Read the Bible history of Abraham and you will discover that before the Lord spoke with him and called him, he worshipped idols **(Joshua 24:2).**

Abraham is not introduced as a perfect man or as one who earned God's favor through works. Instead, **Paul reminds us of what the Scriptures declared:** *"Abraham believed God, and it was counted unto him for righteousness"*

(Romans 4:3).

The term *"counted unto him for righteousness"* means that righteousness was **imputed** to Abraham. To impute is to credit something to another person's account. Think of it like this: if your bank account is empty and someone deposits a million dollars into it, that money is now credited to you, even though you didn't earn it.

In the same way, God placed His righteousness into Abraham's account. Abraham was declared righteous in the sight of God, not because of what he had done, but because of what God placed on his record.

This is the very heart of the gospel. Righteousness is not earned by our efforts but given by God to those who believe. If it were wages, it would be a debt God owed to us. But righteousness is not a paycheck—it is a gift of grace.

Abraham was not justified because of what he did, but because he trusted the God who justifies the ungodly. Paul presses this further by pointing out the timing of Abraham's *justification*.

It happened before circumcision, before the Law, before any outward sign of religion. Abraham's faith was credited to him for righteousness while he was still uncircumcised, so that he could be the father not only of the Jewish people **but of all who believe.**

In this way, Abraham becomes the pattern: righteousness is *imputed by faith,* not by works, ceremonies, or the Law.

This is good news for us. It means that the same God who credited righteousness to Abraham now does the same for us who believe in Jesus Christ.

It is important to understand that there is a difference between believing and having faith.

The difference may seem subtle, but it is significant.

To believe is to accept something as true in the mind; but faith goes further—it acts on that belief and rests its confidence on the Word of God.

Faith has a stronger foundation because it is rooted not in feelings or opinions but in God's promises. Abraham was not merely one who believed in the existence of God—he placed his trust in what God had spoken, and that trust was counted, or imputed, to him as righteousness.

In the same way, we are justified by faith in Christ's death and resurrection. The principle remains the same: grace through faith, not through human striving.

Abraham was **justified by faith** in God's promise; we are justified by faith in Christ's death and resurrection. The principle is the same: grace through faith, not through human striving.

Paul describes Abraham's faith with great detail. Abraham knew the facts—his body was old; Sarah's womb was barren—but he did not allow unbelief to weaken him.

Instead, he believed against hope, fully persuaded that what God had promised, He was able to perform.

His faith gave glory to God, not because it ignored reality and the laws of nature, but because it trusted God above reality. Faith does not deny the facts; it declares that God is greater than the facts.

This is what saving faith looks like. It holds to God's promise even when circumstances scream otherwise. It leans not on human strength but on divine ability. Abraham's story shows us that faith is not passive; it is active trust in the God who raises the dead and calls things that are not as though they were.

And Paul reminds us that this story was not written for Abraham's sake alone but for ours also. We too are counted righteous if we believe on Him who raised up Jesus from the dead.

Jesus was delivered for **our sins** and **raised again for our justification**. What Abraham experienced by faith in promise, we experience by faith in Christ. His righteousness is imputed to us, not because of our works, but because we trust in the finished work of Jesus Christ.

This is the foundation of the Christian life. We do not live by our own strength, our own works, or our own ability to keep the Law.

We live by faith—faith in the God who justifies, the Christ who redeems, and the Spirit who empowers. Abraham's life is not just a story from long ago; it is a mirror for us today.

The just shall live by faith, and faith still opens the door to God's righteousness. When we make the decision to live by faith—to trust fully in God and in the death, burial, and resurrection of Jesus Christ—our lives take on a whole new meaning.

Paul tells us in **Romans 6:4** that just as Christ was raised from the dead by the glory of the Father, we also should walk in newness of life.

This means that through faith we are not only forgiven, but we are raised to live a new kind of life—different from what we once knew, different from what once enslaved us.

No longer bound by *sin, depression,* or *the chains* that once held us back, we now walk in **freedom.**

Our old life has been nailed to the cross, and we are not defined by what we used to be. As Paul declares in **2 Corinthians 5:17**, *"Therefore if any man be in Christ, he is a new creature: old things are passed away; behold, all things are become new."*

This is the reality of the believer's life in Christ. The past no longer dictates our future, because the blood of Jesus has broken the power of guilt, shame, and bondage.

We can move forward in confidence, knowing that Jesus died for our sins, that His blood has set us free, and that we now live a new life in Him.

Abraham's story reminds us that faith is not about perfection but about trusting God's promise. His righteousness was not earned but imputed, credited to him because he believed.

And Paul tells us this was written not for his sake alone, but for us also—because the same God who justified Abraham by faith now justifies us through Jesus Christ, who was delivered for our offences and raised for our justification.

To live by faith is to live as a new creation—free to glorify God in our bodies, our minds, and our daily walk. The just shall live by faith, and through that faith, the Spirit of God makes us living testimonies of His saving power, so that the whole world may see and give glory to God!

Reflective Questions:

1. What does Abraham's story teach you about God's grace in calling imperfect people?

2. How would you explain the difference between believing and having faith to someone who is struggling to trust God?

3. In what area of your life do you most need to live *"against hope, believing in hope"* like Abraham did?

4. How does the truth that righteousness is **imputed** (credited) change the way you see yourself before God?

5. In what ways can your life today serve as a living testimony of God's saving power to those around you?

Reflective Summary:

Paul uses Abraham as the pattern of saving faith. He was not justified by works, by outward signs, or by the Law, but by faith in God's promise.

This faith was imputed to him for righteousness, and Paul makes it clear that the same principle applies to us today.

Through faith in Christ's death and resurrection, we too are credited with righteousness and raised to walk in newness of life.

The just shall live by faith—and when we do, our lives become living testimonies that point the world to the glory of God.

Prayer:

Heavenly Father,

Thank You for calling Abraham out of idolatry and making him the father of faith. Thank You for showing us that righteousness is not earned but imputed by faith.

Lord, help me to live not by sight, but by faith in Your promises. Strengthen me to trust You in the face of impossibilities, just as Abraham did.

Let my life reflect the new creation I am in Christ, and may every step I take bring glory to You. The just shall live by faith—and by Your Spirit, I will.

In Jesus' name, Amen.

Chapter 4 – The Stillness Before the Storm

Some people would have you believe that once you accept Christ, life becomes smooth and effortless. I cannot tell you that. Accepting Jesus Christ as Lord and Savior is simple—it is a gift, freely received by faith. But growing in that faith is a process, one that will test your endurance, your obedience, and even your patience in the still moments before the storms of life.

Yet, let me also say this: even though the road is hard, it is the best decision anyone can ever make. Nothing compares to the life that comes when you surrender to Jesus Christ.

But here is the truth that must be told: you cannot grow in faith without following the pattern God Himself laid out in the New Testament. The steps are clear, and they are not optional.

1. Accept Jesus Christ as Lord and Savior **(Romans 10:9–10).**

2. Plant yourself in a church that is preaching and teaching the truth of the Gospel **(Acts 2:42).**

3. Attend church as often as you can without fail, because it is in the gathering of believers that our faith is stirred, our hearts are strengthened, and our minds are renewed **(John 8:31–32).**

4. Be filled with the Holy Ghost **(Luke 11:13; Acts 2:4; Ephesians 5:18).**

5. Fellowship with men and women mature in the faith **(Hebrews 10:25).**

6. Study God's Word daily and live right **(2 Timothy 2:15; Romans 12:1–2).**

These are not works of the flesh, as some religions use to try to earn God's favor. These are works of the Spirit—marks of a life that has been transformed by grace.

Faith in the Stillness

When I first gave my life to Christ, I thought everything would fall into place immediately. But what I discovered was that God often uses the still seasons—the pauses, the waiting rooms, the quiet places—to test our faith and prepare us for greater storms.

I remember the early days after my conversion. I had confessed Christ, but I did not yet know the importance of being grounded in a Bible-believing church. I thought I could make it on excitement and emotion alone.

That worked for a little while, but soon I found myself weak, distracted, and vulnerable to old temptations. Without the Word, without fellowship, and without the Spirit's power, I was like a soldier without armor.

**It was in that season that God taught me
something vital:** faith is not a feeling; it is a
discipline. Just as the military trained me in
drills, formations, and orders, God began training
me in prayer, Scripture, and obedience. The
stillness was not punishment—it was preparation.

Filled for the Fight

The greatest turning point came when I sought
and received the baptism of the Holy Ghost.

Until then, I was trying to live my life with my
own strength. But once the Spirit filled me, I
experienced power and boldness to testify, and
discernment I never had before.

Still, even after that experience, growth required more than a single encounter. It required discipline. I had to choose to stay in fellowship with saints who were seasoned in the faith. I had to open my Bible when my flesh wanted to stay asleep. I had to confess sin when I wanted to hide.

This was not easy. Faith never is. But it was necessary.

Living Out Faith Through Obedience

Faith is not only about believing; it is about walking. The Bible says, *"Faith without works is dead"* **(James 2:26).** These works are not works of the flesh, where we try to earn salvation by effort. Instead, they are works of the Spirit—acts of obedience that keep us aligned with God's will and open to His blessing.

One of the clearest examples is tithing. The tithe is not just about money—it is about trust. When we bring our ten percent to God's house, we are declaring that everything we have belongs to Him. **Malachi 3:10** reminds us: *"Bring ye all the tithes into the storehouse, that there may be meat in mine house, and prove me now herewith, saith the Lord of hosts, if I will not open you the windows of heaven, and pour you out a blessing, that there shall not be room enough to receive it."*

When I first began walking with the Lord, I struggled with this. Money was tight, and every dollar seemed like it had a place to go. But I learned that if I wanted to walk by faith, I had to trust God with my resources. Every time I honored Him with my tithe, He honored me with provision. Some months I could not explain how the bills were paid, but they were. Tithing trained me not only to give, but to trust.

But tithing is just one part of the life of obedience. There are other disciplines that make your faith effective:

- **Prayer**: Not just a quick word before meals, but a daily conversation with God. Prayer strengthens the believer's inner man and tunes our ears to the Spirit **(1 Thessalonians 5:17).**

- **Fasting:** A forgotten weapon in many churches. Fasting humbles the flesh so that the Spirit may rise in power **(Matthew 6:16–18).**

- **Serving in the church:** Faith grows when it is exercised. Greeting, teaching, helping the poor—all of these stretch your faith and build humility **(Galatians 5:13).**

- **Witnessing:** Sharing your testimony with others. Each time you open your mouth about Christ, you are exercising your faith and pushing back against fear **(Romans 1:16).**

- **Living holy**: Setting your body apart as a temple for the Holy Ghost **(1 Corinthians 6:19–20).** Holiness is not optional; it is evidence that faith is real.

These are not *"extra-credit"* actions. They are the building blocks of a strong Christian life. If you neglect them, your faith will weaken. If you practice them, your faith will grow roots that no storm can shake.

A Command, a Choice, and a Miracle

Through my years of experience, I have come to realize that the Holy Ghost and the Word of God always work in harmony to produce faith. As Paul wrote, *"So then faith cometh by hearing, and hearing by the word of God"* **(Romans 10:17)**. This was not just a verse on a page for me — it became a living reality.

For years, I worked a dead-end government job where merit took a back seat to nepotism. I had all the qualifications for management, but for reasons I could not explain, the glass ceiling refused to break. It was frustrating. My credentials said one thing, but the system said another.

Yet in that season of stagnation, God was building something deeper in me: *the discipline to listen, the courage to obey, and the faith to trust Him beyond what I could see.*

One Tuesday evening in **March of 2017,** as I pulled up in front of my church to drop off those riding with me for Bible study, when I pulled up in front of the church, I distinctly without a doubt heard the voice of the Lord. It was not a whisper; it was a clear command. All He said was one long, drawn-out word: **"Retire."**

I had heard His voice before and hesitated to obey, but this time I knew I could not delay. I turned to those in the car and told them, "The Lord just said to me, **"Retire."** Whether they believed me or not did not matter. From that moment forward, my responsibility was not to convince anyone but to obey what I had heard.

Retirement was not on my radar. It made no sense financially or professionally. But I had learned that God never gives a command without also providing the grace to carry it out.

If He told me to retire, I believed He would take care of all my needs — and that is exactly what He did.

This was not *"name it and claim it"* heresy taught in some churches today. This was not presumption or assumption. This was the Holy Ghost speaking, and me acting in obedience.

One simple step of faith released God's provision in ways I could not have orchestrated. Bills were paid. Opportunities opened. Peace replaced anxiety. All my needs were met, not because I manipulated Scripture, but because I trusted the God who spoke it.

That moment solidified a lesson in my heart: faith is not merely believing the Word, but obeying the Word. It is not just hearing, but hearing and doing **(James 1:22).**

When the Spirit speaks, your responsibility is to obey — and when you obey, His provision follows.

The Hard Road, the Holy Road

Living by faith is not easy, and we must not pretend that it is. There will be setbacks, seasons of silence, unanswered questions, and storms that threaten to break you. I have walked through all of these. But in every test, I have found God faithful.

Salvation is free, but discipleship costs you everything. The flesh resists it, the devil opposes it, and the world mocks it. Yet the reward is eternal life, peace that surpasses understanding, and the presence of the Holy Ghost walking with you every step of the way.

So let me be clear: this is the narrow path. It is not easy, but it is right. And if you walk it faithfully, you will find that God's grace does not just save—it sustains, protects, provides, equips, and transforms you.

The storms will come, but the stillness before them is where your roots go deep. And once your roots are in Christ, nothing in this world can pull you out of His hand.

Reflective Questions:

1. Have I been treating faith as a feeling, or as a daily discipline?

2. Which of the New Testament steps (salvation, church fellowship, Spirit baptism, accountability, Word study) do I need to strengthen in my life right now?

3. Am I consistently honoring God with my tithe and trusting Him with my resources?

4. Which spiritual discipline—prayer, fasting, serving, witnessing, or holiness— do I need to grow in?

5. How can I use this season of stillness to prepare my faith for the storms ahead?

Reflective Summary:

Faith is not an easy walk, but it is the only walk that leads to life. Salvation is free, yet the journey of discipleship requires daily surrender and obedience to the Spirit.

We do not grow strong in Christ by accident— we grow by following the clear pattern God has given: *accepting Jesus as Lord, being planted in a truth-preaching church, being filled with the Holy Ghost, fellowshipping with mature believers, studying and living the Word, and faithfully attending the house of God.*

Added to these, obedience in tithing, prayer, fasting, serving, witnessing, and living holy ensures that our faith is not shallow but deeply rooted.

The stillness before the storm is never wasted. It is the season where roots are tested, faith is stretched, and trust in God becomes real. If you endure in these disciplines, you will discover that the grace of God does more than save—it *sustains, protects, provides, equips, and transforms.*

Though the narrow path is hard, it is the right path, and it will carry you safely through every storm into the everlasting arms of Christ.

A Prayer for Growth in Faith:

Lord Jesus,

I thank You for saving me by grace through faith.

Today I confess that walking by faith has not always been easy, but I believe it is worth it.

Teach me to follow the pattern of Your Word—to stay in fellowship, to be filled with the Spirit, to honor You with my giving, and to live a life of prayer, holiness, and obedience.

Plant my roots deep in You, so that when the storms come, I will stand unshaken.

In Jesus' name, Amen.

Chapter 5 – Faith Under Pressure

Faith will always be tested. Pressure reveals what is real and what is only surface. The Apostle Paul reminds us in **Romans 5:1–5** that because we are *justified by faith*, we have peace with God through our Lord Jesus Christ.

Yet he does not stop there—he also says that we *"glory in tribulations,"* because *tribulations produce patience, patience produces character, and character produces hope.*

This is where many Christians stumble. We rejoice in peace, but we resist *tribulation.* We want God's blessings, but not the pressure that builds endurance.

We want miracles without molding, triumph without testing, and crowns without crosses. But the truth is this: faith under pressure becomes stronger faith.

When Everything Fell Apart

Decades earlier, one of the deepest pressures I faced came after the collapse of my marriage to Kelly. Divorce is never easy, but for me, it was devastating.

I walked away from five years of marriage to a person who was not truly devoted to the marriage and twelve years of military service with nothing to show for it but broken pieces.

Instead of moving forward with honor, I found myself moving back in with my parents, carrying regret and shame like heavy baggage.

I remember lying awake at night thinking, *"This isn't how my life was supposed to turn out."* I had tried to build a future, and instead I found myself living in the past, haunted by what I had lost. The weight of failure pressed hard on me. To many, it looked like my story was over.

I found myself depressed, psychologically unstable, lonely, broke, and uneducated — with no one to lean on and no one to believe my side of the story.

The people I thought would stand by me were silent. Friends disappeared. Family could not understand. My reputation was tarnished, and my heart was shattered.

But God wasn't finished. In that dark season, I learned one of the hardest but most important lessons of my life: you cannot put your trust in people, not even in family—you must put your trust in Jesus only.

My mother and father loved me deeply, but they could not heal the wound. They could not remove the shame. They could not rebuild the broken pieces. Only Jesus could do that.

Shaped in the Fire of Regret

At the time, I thought God had abandoned me. But in truth, He was molding and shaping me.

Regret became the fire, shame became the weight, and loneliness became the chisel in the Master's hand.

He was carving out pride, stripping away self-reliance, and drawing me closer to Himself.

It was in that season that I was broken more than I had ever been. Truthfully, I did not run to my Bible the way some might think I should have. I was too wounded, too consumed with trying to piece myself back together after that devastating divorce and the bitter loss of my boys.

I was hurt for a long time. In my pain, I even turned to women, hoping they could fill the emptiness inside me. But instead of healing me, they only let me down further—mentally, emotionally, and spiritually.

What I wanted was relief. What I wanted were answers. What I wanted was an easy way out of the pain. But God had something deeper in mind.

He used that dark season to teach me patience when I wanted quick solutions, endurance when I wanted escape, and growth when all I wanted was comfort. I could not always feel Him near, but I would later understand that even in my lowest and loneliest moments, He was closer than I had ever realized.

Biblical Patterns of Pressure

I came to understand that what I experienced was not unusual. **Joseph** was thrown into *a pit, sold into slavery, and forgotten in prison,* yet God used that pressure to prepare him to save a nation.

Job lost everything—children, possessions, and health—yet God restored him double. **Paul** was beaten, shipwrecked, and chained, yet he wrote letters that still feed the church today.

In every case, pressure looked like punishment, but it was really preparation. And in every case, faith under pressure produced hope.

Faith Under Pressure Produces Hope

If you are reading this in a season where it feels like God is silent, where every prayer seems unanswered, and where everything you built has fallen apart, know this: you are not abandoned—you are being shaped.

The potter does not leave the clay in the fire to destroy it but to strengthen it. The sculptor does not chisel the stone to harm it but to reveal what is hidden inside.

In the same way, God uses pressure to bring out patience, patience to bring out character, and character to bring out hope.

Faith under pressure is not easy. It strips you down, it hurts, and it leaves scars. But those scars are not signs of defeat—they are reminders that you survived. And more than that, they are proof that God's grace can sustain you through the fire.

Reflective Questions:

1. What pressures in my life right now are testing my faith?

2. Do I see pressure as abandonment, or can I trust that God is molding and shaping me through it?

3. In seasons of regret and shame, have I turned to Jesus as my only anchor, or have I leaned too much on people?

4. How can I allow pressure to build patience, character, and hope in me instead of bitterness?

5. What biblical example of faith under pressure (Joseph, Job, Paul, etc.) speaks most to my current season?

Reflective Summary:

Faith under pressure is not the end of your story; it is the beginning of God reshaping you.

Pressure will come in many forms—*emotional, financial, spiritual, and relational.* It will strip you, test you, and leave you questioning.

But if you hold on, you will see that God never abandons His children. He uses the fire of regret, the weight of shame, and the silence of unanswered prayers to mold us into vessels He can use.

Your faith may feel fragile now, but under pressure it will grow stronger. What looks like punishment may be preparation. What looks like the end may be the very place where God is writing a new beginning.

A Prayer for Endurance:

Lord Jesus,

You know the weight of my heart, the shame of my failures, and the pressures that surround me. I confess that sometimes I feel abandoned, but I choose to trust that You are shaping me for Your glory.

Strengthen me to endure the fire, to hold steady in the silence, and to let You form patience, character, and hope in me. Help me lean not on family, friends, or even my own understanding, but on You alone.

Remind me that even under pressure, You are faithful, and Your grace will sustain me.

In Jesus' name, Amen.

Chapter 6 – The Storm Arrives

Storms do not come without warning. Often, the sky darkens, the wind shifts, and the stillness before the downpour gives us a hint that trouble is near.

Spiritually, it is the same. After seasons of stillness and growth, after learning to endure pressure and trust God's hand, there comes a time when the clouds of trial gather and the storm itself break loose.

I thought I had already lived through the worst storm of my life. Divorce had shattered my home. The loss of my boys had crushed my spirit. The silence of family and friends had nearly destroyed my confidence.

But storms are not polite—they rarely come one at a time. When I was still trying to catch my breath, another storm was already gathering on the horizon.

The enemy does not fight fair. He waits until you are weak, then he strikes harder. Just when I thought I was beginning to rebuild, temptations came back stronger. Betrayals cut deeper. Loneliness pressed heavier. Financial strain returned like an unrelenting wave.

It felt like everything I had tried to stand on was washing away beneath me.

This was no light rain. This was a storm that shook the core of who I was. Nights of pacing the floor, talking to God but hearing nothing back. Days of plastering a smile on my face, only to fall apart in private.

Shame whispered in my ear: *"You will never recover. God has left you. This is who you are now."*

Paul's Storm Within

The apostle Paul described his own storm in **Romans 7**. It was not a storm of weather, but of war—an inner war between his redeemed spirit and his sinful flesh.

"For the good that I would I do not: but the evil which I would not, that I do" **(Romans 7:19).**

Even Paul, the great apostle and teacher of the gospel, confessed to this struggle. On one side was his desire to serve God with all his heart; on the other was the relentless pull of the flesh.

The storm raged within him until he cried out, *"O wretched man that I am! who shall deliver me from the body of this death?"*

(Romans 7:24).

Every believer who has walked with God for any length of time knows this storm. It is not fought with umbrellas and shelters but with *prayer, fasting, and the power of the Holy Ghost.*

My Own Storms

When the storm arrived in my life, it hit harder than I imagined. Betrayals came from those I trusted most. Temptations I thought I had mastered returned with greater force. Finances collapsed again. Emotional wounds reopened.

There were nights when I could not sleep, pacing the floor, asking God if He had forgotten me.

There were mornings I rose weary, carrying shame that whispered, *"You will never recover from this."* Like Paul, I felt the war inside me— my spirit wanting to obey, but my flesh wanting to run.

It was during this time that I learned storms have a way of stripping away the superficial. A storm will expose whether your faith is rooted in feelings or in the unshakable Word of God.

A storm will reveal whether you are anchored in Christ or drifting on the sea of your own strength.

The Anchor in the Storm

But storms are not the end of the story. Paul didn't stop with despair. He turned to hope: *"I thank God through Jesus Christ our Lord"*

(Romans 7:25).

And then he declared the verse that has held me in my darkest hours: *"There is therefore now no condemnation to them which are in Christ Jesus, who walk not after the flesh, but after the Spirit"*

(Romans 8:1).

The storm told me I was condemned, but the Word told me I was covered. The storm told me I was forgotten, but the Word told me I was chosen. The storm told me I was weak, but the Spirit whispered, *"My grace is sufficient for thee: for my strength is made perfect in weakness"* **(2 Corinthians 12:9).**

When the waves rose, I clung to promises like:

- *"When thou passest through the waters, I will be with thee; and through the rivers, they shall not overflow thee"* **(Isaiah 43:2).**

- *"The Lord also will be a refuge for the oppressed, a refuge in times of trouble"* **(Psalm 9:9).**

- *"God is our refuge and strength, a very present help in trouble"* **(Psalm 46:1).**

These were not just verses on a page—they were lifelines in the storm.

God's Purpose in the Storm

Why does God allow storms? Not to destroy us, but to deepen us. *"My brethren, count it all joy when ye fall into divers temptations; knowing this, that the trying of your faith worketh patience"* **(James 1:2–3).**

Storms are the proving ground of faith. Just as a tree's roots grow deeper when the winds press against it, so our faith grows stronger when the storms rage around us. **Tribulations,** Paul says, *"produce patience; and patience, experience; and experience, hope"* **(Romans 5:3–4).**

In the storm, God was carving out pride, teaching me dependence, and showing me that the Spirit's power is greater than my flesh's weakness.

Paul's cry in **Romans 7** does not end in despair—it ends in victory: *"I thank God through Jesus Christ our Lord."* The storm may rage, but Jesus remains the anchor **(Hebrews 6:19).**

Lessons from the Storm

I came out of those seasons battered, but not broken; wounded, but wiser. And what I learned, I now share with you:

- **Storms are inevitable.** You cannot pray them away, but you can prepare for them **(John 16:33).**

- **Storms test your foundation.** If your roots are in Christ, you will stand **(Matthew 7:24–25).**

- **Storms are temporary.** The night may be long, but the dawn always comes **(Psalm 30:5).**

- **Storms make you stronger.** What you survive, God will use to shape and send you **(2 Corinthians 4:17).**

Like Paul, I learned to confess not only my weakness but also Christ's strength. For it is in the storm that His grace proves sufficient and His power is made perfect in weakness.

And that is why I can say now: the storm did not come to kill me. It came to reveal Christ in me.

Reflective Questions:

1. What storms in your life have tested your foundation in Christ, and what did they reveal about where your faith truly rests?

2. When shame and guilt whisper lies in the middle of your storm, how can **Romans 8:1** strengthen your heart?

3. Which Scriptures have become your lifeline during times of trial, the way **Isaiah 43:2** or **Psalm 46:1** were for me?

4. In what ways has God used storms to strip away false supports and draw you closer to Him?

5. How can you prepare now, in the still moments, so that when storms come you remain anchored in Christ?

Reflective Summary:

Storms come to every believer, but they are not signs of abandonment—they are classrooms of faith. Paul admitted his own inner storm in **Romans 7,** but he also declared the victory of **Romans 8:1**: *"There is therefore now no condemnation to them which are in Christ Jesus."*

The storms of life will expose weakness, reveal what we are leaning on, and test whether our roots go down deep into Christ. Yet in those moments, the Word of God becomes more than ink on paper; it becomes the very anchor of our soul **(Hebrews 6:19).**

What the enemy intends to use for destruction, God uses for transformation. The storm does not come to kill us—it comes to reveal Christ in us, to deepen our patience, strengthen our character, and increase our hope **(Romans 5:3–4).**

A Prayer for Strength in the Storm:

Heavenly Father,

I thank You that even in the fiercest storms of life, You remain my anchor. When the winds rage and shame whispers lies, remind me of Your Word: *that there is no condemnation for those who are in Christ Jesus.* Strengthen my faith when I feel weak, and let Your grace be sufficient when my strength fails.

Teach me to count it all joy when trials come, knowing that You are shaping me through them. Help me to cling to Your promises—that You will never leave me nor forsake me, that *You are my refuge and strength, a very present help in trouble.*

Lord, let the storms of my life not drive me away from You, but deeper into Your presence. Use them to strip away pride, false supports, and fear, until all that remains is Christ in me, the hope of glory.

In Jesus' name, Amen.

Chapter 7 – Life in the Spirit

Romans 8 is the mountaintop of Paul's letter to the Romans. After the battle of **chapter 7,** where he cried, *"O wretched man that I am!"* we now hear his victorious declaration: *"There is therefore now no condemnation to them which are in Christ Jesus, who walk not after the flesh, but after the Spirit"* **(Romans 8:1).**

This is the turning point for every believer. The storms of guilt, shame, and condemnation rage until the Spirit of God comes in and declares a new verdict: *"Not guilty. Forgiven. Free."*

What the Law could not do, because our flesh was weak, God accomplished through Jesus Christ. And now, through His Spirit, we are empowered to live a life that pleases God.

Filled With the Spirit

It is not enough to simply know about Jesus or to agree with doctrine in our minds. To walk in victory, we must be filled with the Holy Spirit.

Paul writes, *"If any man have not the Spirit of Christ, he is none of his"* **(Romans 8:9).** The Spirit is not optional—it is the seal of our salvation, the source of our strength, and the evidence that we belong to Christ.

When I tried to live this life without being filled, I found myself defeated again and again. My flesh wanted control. Temptations were strong, and my willpower was weak.

But the moment I was filled with the Spirit, everything in my life began to shift. It did not happen overnight, but God started stripping away the things I thought were important and precious—friends, habits, desires, and even relationships that were holding me back. At first, it felt like loss, but I came to understand it was really freedom.

There was now a power at work in me greater than my flesh, greater than my willpower, greater than my weakness. Jesus had promised this when He said, *"But ye shall receive power, after that the Holy Ghost is come upon you"* **(Acts 1:8).** That power was no longer just a verse I heard in church—it became a reality in my daily life.

The filling of the Spirit is not just about speaking in tongues, though that is the biblical evidence **(Acts 2:4).** It is about being saturated with God's presence until His desires become your desires, His strength becomes your strength, and His holiness becomes your pursuit.

Paul exhorted the Ephesians, *"Be not drunk with wine, wherein is excess; but be filled with the Spirit"* **(Ephesians 5:18).** Notice he did not say "be filled once," but spoke of a continual filling.

Jesus Himself explained the necessity of this life in the Spirit: *"He that believeth on me, as the scripture hath said, out of his belly shall flow rivers of living water. (But this spake he of the Spirit, which they that believe on him should receive)"* **(John 7:38–39).**

The Spirit is not a trickle—it is rivers of life, flowing out of the believer to impact the world.

Led by the Spirit

But it is not enough to be filled once. The Spirit must also lead us daily. Paul writes, *"For as many as are led by the Spirit of God, they are the sons of God"* **(Romans 8:14).** Notice the word led. This means the Spirit is not a guest in our lives—**He is the Guide.**

He directs our steps, convicts us when we wander, and gives us discernment when choices are unclear. As Jesus said, *"Howbeit when he, the Spirit of truth, is come, he will guide you into all truth"* **(John 16:13).**

I had to learn this the hard way. When I tried to lead myself, I ended up in broken places, repeating old mistakes, listening to the lies of the enemy.

But when I yielded and allowed the Spirit to lead me—through *prayer, fasting, and obedience*—things began to change.

It did not happen all at once, but step by step, the Spirit guided me into a new way of living. He led me out of destructive relationships that drained me, out of destructive habits that bound me, and into a life marked by peace, purpose, and clarity.

This is exactly what Paul meant when he wrote, *"This I say then, Walk in the Spirit, and ye shall not fulfil the lust of the flesh"* **(Galatians 5:16).**

To walk in the Spirit is to take one step at a time under His direction, trusting that His guidance is greater than our own understanding.

Jesus Himself promised that the Spirit would be our teacher and guide: *"Howbeit when he, the Spirit of truth, is come, he will guide you into all truth"* **(John 16:13).**

When I learned to follow His lead, I discovered that the Spirit not only pulled me out of what was destroying me, but also pushed me into what was destined for me.

The flesh pulls one way, but the Spirit leads another. *"For to be carnally minded is death; but to be spiritually minded is life and peace"* **(Romans 8:6).** That "life and peace" is the mark of a Spirit-led believer.

Paul warned the Galatians, *"This I say then, Walk in the Spirit, and ye shall not fulfil the lust of the flesh"* **(Galatians 5:16).** Flesh and Spirit are always at war, but the Spirit gives victory when we yield.

The Spirit in Our Weakness

Even after being filled and led, there are moments when we do not know what to pray, when weakness overwhelms us.

But Paul assures us, *"Likewise the Spirit also helpeth our infirmities: for we know not what we should pray for as we ought: but the Spirit itself maketh intercession for us with groanings which cannot be uttered"* **(Romans 8:26).**

This means the Spirit is not only with us in our victories but also in our weakness. He prays through us, strengthens us when words fail, and carries us when we cannot carry ourselves.

Jude 20 tells us, *"But ye, beloved, building up yourselves on your most holy faith, praying in the Holy Ghost."* Spirit-led prayer builds us up when everything else is tearing us down.

The Spirit of Adoption

And here is one of the greatest works of the Spirit: He assures us that we are children of God. *"For ye have not received the spirit of bondage again to fear; but ye have received the Spirit of adoption, whereby we cry, Abba, Father"* **(Romans 8:15).**

Fear once controlled me. I felt like an orphan, ashamed, abandoned and overlooked. But when the Spirit filled me, I understood that I was not forsaken—I was adopted.

God Himself had claimed me as His child. That assurance silenced the lies of the enemy and gave me boldness to walk as a son, not as a slave. Paul writes in **Galatians 4:6,** *"And because ye are sons, God hath sent forth the Spirit of his Son into your hearts, crying, Abba, Father."*

The Spirit is the witness that we belong to God. As **Ephesians 1:13–14** declares, *"In whom also after that ye believed, ye were sealed with that holy Spirit of promise, Which is the earnest of our inheritance until the redemption of the purchased possession."* The Spirit is both our seal and our guarantee.

Key Truth

The victorious Christian life is not possible without the Holy Ghost. Being filled once is not enough—we must continually be led by the Spirit. Without Him, we drift back into the flesh. With Him, we walk in life, peace, power, identity, and victory.

Reflective Questions:

1. What areas of your life still resist the Spirit's filling, and how can you surrender them to God?

2. How does **Galatians 5:16** challenge you to "walk in the Spirit" in your daily choices?

3. In what ways has the Spirit led you away from destructive habits or relationships, and how did that leadership bring peace?

4. How does the Spirit's role as Comforter **(John 14:26)** give you hope in times of weakness?

5. What practical steps **(prayer, fasting, obedience)** can you take to cultivate a lifestyle of being filled and led by the Spirit?

Reflective Summary:

Life in the Spirit is not a one-time experience; it is a continual walk of surrender and renewal. To be filled with the Spirit is to receive the power Jesus promised in **Acts 1:8**, a power greater than our flesh and stronger than our willpower.

To be led by the Spirit is to submit each day to His direction, step by step, trusting that He will guide us into all truth **(John 16:13).**

The Spirit frees us from condemnation, strengthens us in weakness, and assures us that we are sons and daughters of God.

As Paul wrote, *"For as many as are led by the Spirit of God, they are the sons of God"* **(Romans 8:14).**

This is our identity and our inheritance. The Spirit not only rescues us from what destroys us but ushers us into what God has destined for us—life, peace, and victory.

Prayer:

Heavenly Father,

Your Word declares that if we ask, You will give the Holy Spirit to those who hunger and thirst for Him **(Luke 11:13).**

Lord, I come before You on behalf of every person reading these words who longs to be filled with the Holy Ghost.

Pour out Your Spirit upon them. Break the chains of fear, guilt, and doubt, and open their hearts to receive Your promise.

Let the rivers of living water that Jesus spoke of in **John 7:38** flow freely in their lives. Baptize them with power from on high, just as You did for the believers in **Acts 2,** so they may walk in *victory, boldness, and holiness.*

Father, let this moment be the turning point where condemnation ends and freedom begins.

Fill them until every part of their being is saturated with Your presence. Lead them daily, strengthen them in weakness, and seal them as Your children.

We ask this in faith, in the mighty name of Jesus, Amen.

Chapter 8 – More Than Conquerors

Paul lifts our eyes in **Romans 8** from the struggle of the flesh to the victory of the Spirit. After declaring that there is no condemnation for those who are in Christ, he now shows us that there is also no defeat for those who walk in Him.

"For I reckon that the sufferings of this present time are not worthy to be compared with the glory which shall be revealed in us" **(Romans 8:18).**

This is a perspective only the Spirit can give. The storms of life may rage, suffering may pierce us, and trials may seem unending, but in Christ, suffering is never the end of the story. Glory is coming. Hope is waiting. Victory is assured.

I had to learn this in my own journey. There were moments when pain and betrayal tempted me to believe the storm would last forever.

But the Spirit reminded me that every trial has an expiration date, and every tear is counted by God. What felt unbearable in the moment was producing something eternal in me.

Paul explains it elsewhere: *"For our light affliction, which is but for a moment, worketh for us a far more exceeding and eternal weight of glory"* **(2 Corinthians 4:17).**

God's Purpose in All Things

Perhaps one of the most comforting promises in all of Scripture is found here: *"And we know that all things work together for good to them that love God, to them who are the called according to his purpose"* **(Romans 8:28).**

Notice Paul does not say all things are good. Betrayal is not good. Pain is not good. Storms are not good. But God weaves even the worst things into His greater purpose.

When I looked back on my storms, I began to see that what the enemy meant for evil, God was using for my good **(Genesis 50:20).**

If God Be for Us

Paul drives the point home with a question that silences every doubt: *"What shall we then say to these things? If God be for us, who can be against us?"* **(Romans 8:31).**

Those words are not theory to me — they are my testimony.

Years ago, while working at the VA hospital in Brecksville, the Spirit warned me one evening: *"They are going to fire you."* Days later, it happened exactly as the Lord had spoken. I was stunned, terminated without explanation, left to fight back on my own.

For seven long months, I went through every channel I could — the union, the U.S. Equal Employment Opportunity Commission (EEOC), the U.S. Merit Protection Board, even my Congresswoman — but nothing worked.

I was weary, but one day after class, the Spirit nudged me: "Gather your things and go across the street." Across the street stood Cleveland-Marshall College of Law. I had never thought to go there, but God was leading me to help.

That moment became the turning point. The Lord raised up the legal support I needed, and eventually my job was not only restored, but elevated — with a better location, a better position, and back pay. And most of all, I did not have to pay a single dime in legal fees. What man thought was the end, God turned into another beginning.

That season taught me a lesson I will never forget: how people treat others can have spiritual consequences. This isn't pride speaking; it's a testimony. When God places His hand on someone's life, mistreating them is not just unkind—it is dangerous ground. His Word declares, *"Touch not mine anointed, and do my prophets no harm"* **(Psalm 105:15).**

When the VA terminated me, they thought they were simply dismissing an employee. But in reality, they were touching someone God had *called, justified, and sealed by His Spirit.* And when God is for you, it truly does not matter who stands against you, because *"No weapon that is formed against thee shall prosper"* **(Isaiah 54:17).**

A Call to Handle With Care

They assumed I was ordinary—someone they could overlook, use, or discard at will. What they didn't realize was that they were mishandling a divine assignment. I was not just a relative, a coworker, or a friend; I was a conduit of grace, a carrier of God's favor, and a living connection to His healing and provision.

God had strategically placed me in their path as a lifeline. Instead of honoring that, they mocked it, rejected it, or minimized it. Scripture is clear: *"He that heareth you heareth me; and he that despiseth you despiseth me"* **(Luke 10:16).**

Regret always follows dishonor. Many do not realize what they had until the covering lifts, the favor fades, or the peace departs. They thought they were merely walking away from me; in truth, they were walking away from a blessing God had packaged through me. *"He that receiveth a prophet in the name of a prophet shall receive a prophet's reward"* **(Matthew 10:41).**

When you mishandle the messenger, you also mishandle the reward that comes with the message.

Spiritual Consequences of Dishonor

Some people arrive in our lives as heaven's assignment—people marked with a *"handle with care"* warning. I am one of those. I don't say it to boast, but to bear witness: I didn't show up by accident. I was sent, intentionally and quietly, by God. Because I did not come wrapped in prestige or status, they mistook the weight I carried and disrespected the grace they were benefiting from.

And now the fruit of their choices speaks louder than my absence. The favor they enjoyed while connected to me is gone. The peace they once felt has been disrupted. The unseen covering that sheltered them has been lifted. God's promise still stands: *"I will bless them that bless thee, and curse him that curseth thee"* **(Genesis 12:3).**

You cannot curse what God has blessed, nor prosper while scorning what God has sent. *"No weapon that is formed against thee shall prosper… This is the heritage of the servants of the LORD"* **(Isaiah 54:17).**

They believed they could discard me and *"upgrade,"* but you cannot upgrade from what God Himself has ordained. *"He that toucheth you toucheth the apple of his eye"* **(Zechariah 2:8).**

That is exactly what my ex-wives did, and the same goes for others who came up against me.

They thought that leaving me or opposing me would bring them an upgrade—an easier life, a better partner, a new opportunity.

But in reality, they were stepping out from under the very grace and protection God had extended to them through my life. They did not realize that when they mishandled me, they were mishandling the blessing God had attached to me.

The truth is this: when you disconnect from a vessel God has chosen, you don't just lose the relationship—you forfeit the divine covering that came with it.

My ex-wives thought they were moving forward, but what they called an *"upgrade"* became a downgrade in the Spirit. The peace, the favor, the blessing, the protection—they all lifted, because the source was never me, but God working through me.

When people mishandle what God has ordained, they do not just lose a person; they lose access to *the grace, healing, and favor* that person carried. And once it is gone, no counterfeit *"upgrade"* can replace it.

Some have *"entertained angels unawares"* **(Hebrews 13:2);** others have dismissed God's servants unaware. Both choices carry consequences.

Hear me: this is not bitterness speaking; it is a warning wrapped in mercy. Honor what God sends, even when it doesn't look like what you imagined.

Receive those He assigns to your life, and the reward attached to their obedience will flow to you **(Matthew 10:40–42).** Resist them, and you resist the grace sent to lift you.

As for me, I remain persuaded—by Scripture and by experience— *"If God be for us, who can be against us?"* **(Romans 8:31).**

I forgive. I release. And I walk on in the love that made me more than a conqueror. What others mishandled, God has held. What others rejected, God has redeemed. And because His love never fails, I keep moving forward—covered, commissioned, and conquering. *"Nay, in all these things we are more than conquerors through him that loved us"* **(Romans 8:37).**

More Than Conquerors

More than conquerors do not mean life will be without battles. It means no battle can defeat us.

It does not mean the absence of pain, but it means pain cannot destroy us. It means that in Christ, every trial becomes a testimony, every storm becomes a stepping stone, and every setback becomes part of the setup for victory.

Paul concludes with words that every believer must cling to: *"For I am persuaded, that neither death, nor life, nor angels, nor principalities, nor powers, nor things present, nor things to come, Nor height, nor depth, nor any other creature, shall be able to separate us from the love of God, which is in Christ Jesus our Lord"* **(Romans 8:38–39).**

This is the anchor of our faith. Nothing can separate us. Not storms. Not suffering. Not even our failures. The love of Christ is unbreakable, unshakable, and eternal. And because of that love, we do not just survive life—we overcome it. We are more than conquerors.

Reflective Questions:

1. When you look back over your life, what trials has God already brought you through that remind you He is making you more than a conqueror?

2. How does **Romans 8:28** encourage you to trust that even painful experiences can be woven into God's greater plan?

3. In what ways have you experienced the truth of **Romans 8:31** — *"If God be for us, who can be against us?"*

4. How can you shift your perspective so that current struggles are seen in light of the *"glory which shall be revealed"* **(Romans 8:18)**?

5. What practical steps can you take to remain persuaded, as Paul was, that nothing can separate you from the love of God in Christ Jesus?

Reflective Summary:

Romans 8 lifts the believer from condemnation to triumph. Life in the Spirit begins with freedom, but it culminates in victory.

The sufferings of this present time are temporary, while the glory God has prepared for His children is eternal.

Our *battles, betrayals, and hardships* are real, but they are also purposeful. God uses every storm to produce *patience, endurance, and hope.*

The testimony of Paul and the testimony of our own lives point to the same truth: *"If God be for us, who can be against us?"*

Opposition may rise, people may fail us, but the love of Christ holds us secure. We are not simply survivors, but overcomers. Through Christ who loves us, we are more than conquerors.

Nothing — not death, not life, not angels, not principalities, not powers — can separate us from His unshakable love. This is our confidence, our heritage, and our eternal victory.

Prayer:

Heavenly Father,

Thank You for the promise that in Christ we are more than conquerors. Lord, I lift up every reader who feels defeated, rejected, or overlooked. Remind them today that Your love is unbreakable and Your presence is unshakable.

Father, let them see that even their current suffering is working toward a greater glory.

Teach them to rest in Your Word that all things work together for good to those who love You.

Strengthen their hearts with the assurance that no weapon formed against them will prosper, and that if You are for them, no one can stand against them.

Holy Spirit, fill them with boldness, surround them with peace, and let the truth of **Romans 8:37** take root: *"Nay, in all these things we are more than conquerors through him that loved us."* May this victory not just be words on a page, but the reality of their lives.

In Jesus' mighty name, Amen.

Chapter 9 – God's Sovereign Mercy

Paul's heart breaks in **Romans 9–11** as he speaks about Israel, his own people. He longs for their salvation and explains the mystery of God's sovereignty. It is here that Paul reminds us that the call of God is not about our effort, our heritage, or our merit — it is about His mercy.

"For he saith to Moses, I will have mercy on whom I will have mercy, and I will have compassion on whom I will have compassion. So then it is not of him that willeth, nor of him that runneth, but of God that sheweth mercy"

(Romans 9:15–16).

This truth is humbling. It means that salvation is not earned by our striving. It is not achieved by works. It is not secured by human approval. It is the gift of God's sovereign grace.

Israel had the promises, the prophets, and the law, yet many stumbled because they sought righteousness by works instead of faith.

Paul writes: *"They stumbled at that stumblingstone; As it is written, Behold, I lay in Sion a stumblingstone and rock of offence: and whosoever believeth on him shall not be ashamed"* **(Romans 9:32–33).** That stumbling stone is Christ.

And yet, Paul shows in **Romans 10** that salvation is near to all: *"That if thou shalt confess with thy mouth the Lord Jesus, and shalt believe in thine heart that God hath raised him from the dead, thou shalt be saved"* **(Romans 10:9).** God's mercy extends beyond Israel to all nations, proving that His promises never fail.

Even today, some reject Him because He does not come in the package they expected. But to those who receive Him by faith, Christ is not a stumbling stone — He is the cornerstone.

The lesson of **Romans 9–11** is clear: God's plan cannot be overturned. His Word cannot fail. His mercy cannot be stopped. He is the God who keeps His covenant, shows compassion to whom He will, and invites all who believe to be grafted into His family.

Reflective Questions:

1. How does **Romans 9:16** *("it is not of him that willeth, nor of him that runneth, but of God that sheweth mercy")* challenge the way you think about salvation?

2. Have you ever tried to earn God's favor through your own works or effort? What does **Romans 10:9–10** teach you about the true path to righteousness?

3. In what ways has Christ been a "stumbling stone" to some, but the cornerstone of your life?

4. Do you see God's mercy in your own story — moments when He pursued you even when you weren't seeking Him?

5. How can you live with greater gratitude, knowing that your salvation is a gift of mercy and not of works?

Reflective Summary:

Romans 9–11 reminds us that salvation is not based on our merit, our background, or our striving. It is wholly the result of God's mercy.

Paul shows us that Israel, though blessed with the promises of God, stumbled because they sought righteousness through works instead of faith. But Christ, the cornerstone, has become the sure foundation for all who believe.

God's mercy extends beyond boundaries, beyond nations, and beyond human expectations. He grafts into His family anyone who will confess with their mouth that Jesus is Lord and believe in their heart that God raised Him from the dead.

His plan cannot fail, His promises cannot be broken, and His mercy cannot be stopped.

The message is clear: salvation is near, and it is available to all who call upon the name of the Lord.

Prayer for Salvation:

Heavenly Father,

I thank You for Your mercy that cannot be earned and for Your grace that cannot be repaid.

Lord, I confess that without You I am lost, but with You I am found. I believe that Jesus Christ is the Son of God, that He died for my sins, and that You raised Him from the dead.

I confess Him now as Lord and Savior of my life. Wash me in Your mercy, fill me with Your Spirit, and graft me into Your family. Thank You for making me a part of Your plan and for saving me by grace through faith.

Help me to walk each day with gratitude, humility, and obedience, remembering that I am saved not by my works, but by Your love.

In Jesus' name, Amen.

Chapter 10 – Living Sacrifices

After walking us through *justification, life in the Spirit, and the sovereignty of God,* Paul now turns to the practical call of faith. **Romans 12** begins with a command that is both simple and all-encompassing:

"I beseech you therefore, brethren, by the mercies of God, that ye present your bodies a living sacrifice, holy, acceptable unto God, which is your reasonable service. And be not conformed to this world: but be ye transformed by the renewing of your mind, that ye may prove what is that good, and acceptable, and perfect, will of God." **(Romans 12:1–2)**

The Christian life is not about offering God part of ourselves while holding back what feels comfortable. It is about yielding completely—body, mind, and spirit—so that His will becomes our way.

Testimony Connection

There was a season in my life when I thought I could carry both the will of God and the desires of the flesh. But every time I stepped outside of His will—especially in relationships—I found nothing but torment, delay, and the loss of peace.

What looked like freedom was really bondage. What looked like love was really deception. The Spirit showed me that compromise always costs more than it promises.

I learned that presenting my body as a living sacrifice meant surrendering even my relationships to God's authority.

Paul said in **1 Corinthians 9:27**, *"But I keep under my body, and bring it into subjection: lest that by any means, when I have preached to others, I myself should be a castaway."* That Scripture became real to me. I could not run this race carrying the weight of disobedience. I had to *discipline my flesh, renew my mind, and submit every area—especially the hidden ones—to the Spirit of God.*

And when I did, I experienced what **Romans 12** promises: *transformation.* No longer conformed to the patterns of this world, no longer enslaved to my own desires, but reshaped into a vessel God could use. That obedience brought me clarity, peace, and a renewed purpose in Christ.

A Life on the Altar

Paul does not ask for a dead sacrifice like those offered on the altar in the Old Testament. He calls for a living sacrifice. That means every part of our daily life—*our words, our thoughts, our choices, our bodies, and our resources*—belongs to God.

Worship is not just what we do in church; it is how we live when no one is watching.

When I finally understood this, I realized Christianity is not just about what God delivers us from—it is about what He calls us to. He calls us to lay ourselves down, not in death, but in obedience.

Transformed, Not Conformed

Paul warns us not to be conformed to this world. The world will always try to shape us in its mold: through culture, pressure, and compromise. But the Spirit calls us to *transformation—a renewing of the mind through God's Word and His Spirit.*

I learned the hard way that when I tried to fit in with the world, I lost my peace. But when I yielded to the Spirit and allowed Him to reshape my mind and desires, I discovered clarity, joy, peace, and purpose.

Serving With Humility

Romans 12 also reminds us that walking by faith is not a solo journey. Paul says, *"For as we have many members in one body, and all members have not the same office: So we, being many, are one body in Christ, and every one members one of another"* **(Romans 12:4–5).**

The Spirit gives gifts to each believer, not for pride, but for service. Whether *prophecy, teaching, serving, encouraging, giving, or leading*—each gift is holy when it is used in humility to build up the Body of Christ.

Love Without Hypocrisy

Paul sums up the Spirit-filled life with one word: love. *"Let love be without dissimulation. Abhor that which is evil; cleave to that which is good"* **(Romans 12:9).** Real love is not fake, shallow, or self-serving. It is patient, humble, forgiving, and sincere.

In my own life, I saw that whenever I acted out of pride or selfishness, my relationships crumbled. But when I loved with sincerity—even when it cost me—the Spirit brought healing and reconciliation.

Reflective Questions:

1. What does it mean to you personally to present your body as a *"living sacrifice"* **(Romans 12:1)**?

2. "In what areas of your life do you feel the world's pressure to conform, and how can making the right decisions to live for God allow the Spirit to renew your mind in those areas?"

3. What spiritual gift(s) has God placed in your life, and how are you using them to build up the Body of Christ?

4. How can you practice sincere love this week — love without hypocrisy — in your family, church, or community?

5. What one thing might God be asking you to lay on the altar today so that you can walk more fully in His will?

Reflective Summary:

Romans 12 calls every believer to a deeper level of commitment: to live as a sacrifice on God's altar, holy and acceptable to Him.

This is not about empty ritual but about daily obedience. True worship is not confined to songs or Sunday services — it is expressed in how we live, how we love, and how we serve.

To live this way, we must be **transformed,** not conformed. The world's mold is shallow and temporary, but the Spirit's work in us is lasting and eternal. Renewal begins in the mind and flows into every part of life.

God has also equipped each believer with spiritual gifts, not to be hidden or misused, but to strengthen the Body of Christ. Whether our gift is *service, encouragement, giving, or leadership,* all are needed and all are sacred.

And above all, Paul reminds us that our witness must be marked by sincere love.

To live as a living sacrifice is to say: "Lord, all I am and all I have belongs to You." This is not extraordinary service — Paul calls it our reasonable service.

Prayer of Dedication:

Heavenly Father,

I thank You for calling me to live as a living sacrifice, holy and acceptable to You. Lord, I lay my life on Your altar today — my thoughts, my desires, my body, and my will. Take all that I am and use it for Your glory.

Transform me by the renewing of my mind. Break every pattern of conformity to this world, and shape me into the image of Your Son.

Teach me to walk in the gifts You have given me with humility and faithfulness, and to use them to bless others and strengthen the Body of Christ.

Above all, fill me with sincere love. Let me abhor what is evil and cleave to what is good. Let my life testify to Your grace, not only in words but in deeds.

I choose today to be a living sacrifice, not out of compulsion, but out of gratitude for Your mercy.

In Jesus' name, Amen.

Chapter 11 – Subjection, Love, and the Light

Paul continues his practical instructions for the Christian life by addressing how believers are to live in relation to governing authorities and one another. The gospel is not only about heaven—it shapes how we live on earth.

Subjection to Authority

Paul begins with a command many struggle with:

"Let every soul be subject unto the higher powers. For there is no power but of God: the powers that be are ordained of God." **(Romans 13:1)**

This does not mean every authority is righteous or godly, but it does mean that God, in His sovereignty, allows structures of authority for order. Christians are called to respect and obey laws as long as they do not contradict God's higher law.

Rebellion against rightful authority ultimately reflects rebellion against God's order. Paul reminds us that rulers are meant to be *"a terror not to good works, but to the evil"* **(v. 3)**. Even when governments or leaders fail, the believer is called to trust that God's sovereignty is greater than human weakness.

Submission and Warfare

Paul's call to subjection in **Romans 13** is not an isolated theme. Peter also reminds believers that submission is part of our spiritual warfare. In his letter he writes:

"Likewise, ye younger, submit yourselves unto the elder. Yea, all of you be subject one to another, and be clothed with humility: for God resisteth the proud, and giveth grace to the humble. Humble yourselves therefore under the mighty hand of God, that he may exalt you in due time: Casting all your care upon him; for he careth for you. Be sober, be vigilant; because your adversary the devil, as a roaring lion, walketh about, seeking whom he may devour."

(1 Peter 5:5–8)

Peter ties submission to *humility, and humility to victory over the enemy*. The devil devours the proud, but he cannot overcome the humble.

Submission is not weakness—it is warfare. To submit is to stand under God's protection, to walk in His order, and to resist the schemes of Satan.

Testimony Connection

I had to learn this in my own life. There were times when I resisted authority out of pride, wanting to prove I was strong enough to stand on my own. Pride felt like strength in the moment, but it only opened doors to warfare I wasn't prepared for.

I confused independence with maturity and boldness with wisdom. Looking back, I can see that some of my hardest battles weren't because the devil was so strong, but because I was so stubborn.

From the very beginning of our marriage, my desire was to protect Jo from the enemy who threatens all of humanity—the devil. I wanted her to see my efforts and appreciate the spiritual covering I was trying to provide.

I understood that true protection in a home comes when everyone learns to submit to one another in the fear of God **(Ephesians 5:21).** But while I longed for her to submit to spiritual authority in the household, I had to learn that submission is not something you demand—it is something you model by leading with humility and love.

The truth is, I had once again married the wrong woman for the season and calling God had placed on my life. Jo was not willing to yield to spiritual order, and that created constant friction in the home. My intentions were to cover and protect her, but without humility those efforts often turned into tension instead of peace.

Conversations that could have ended in minutes stretched into heated arguments, because I was unwilling to humble myself and listen to the counsel of Pastor Gwendolyn McCurry. She warned me plainly not to marry Jo, telling me that she was not sent from God but was a hindrance to my God-given mission.

Instead of receiving that word with humility, I pushed past it in pride, believing I could make the marriage work on my own strength.

The enemy thrives in that kind of atmosphere—
when godly counsel is ignored, when pride
drowns out wisdom, and when strife takes the
place of peace.

The devil doesn't always need to destroy a man
with outside attacks; sometimes he uses
disobedience and a deaf ear to truth to open the
door. And that was exactly what happened. The
lack of spiritual agreement in my home gave the
enemy room to sow division, frustration, and
weariness.

Peace left the room when pride entered it. But
when I finally chose humility—by softening my
answers, practicing repentance, and admitting
that I had missed God's warning—healing slowly
began to take place. **Proverbs 15:1** became real
to me: *"A soft answer turneth away wrath: but
grievous words stir up anger."*

The Spirit showed me that ignoring wise counsel will always cost more than listening, and humility is the only way to close the door the enemy uses to enter.

In the military, I learned the power of a chain of command. You don't survive long second-guessing lawful orders on the battlefield. What seemed small—uniform, formation, timing—was actually training my soul to obey quickly.

That discipline saved me spiritually later. Submission isn't weakness; it's strength under control. When I carried that posture into my walk with God, I found the same thing to be true: *order brings covering, and covering brings safety.*

There is a spiritual principle at work here. Pride breaks rank and creates gaps; the enemy looks for those gaps. Scripture says, *"God resisteth the proud, and giveth grace to the humble"* **(1 Peter 5:5).**

When I stood in pride, I stood where God resists. When I humbled myself, I stood where grace flows. And right after that call to humility, Peter warns us to *be sober and vigilant because the adversary is seeking whom he may devour* **(1 Peter 5:8)**.

Pride makes you devourable; humility makes you defendable.

Submission also shut down anxiety in my life. Peter says, *"Casting all your care upon him; for he careth for you"* **(1 Peter 5:7).**

I used to carry battles God never asked me to fight—trying to control outcomes at home, at church, and on the job. When I submitted those areas back to God, I stopped carrying what only He can hold. The proof of submission is not just obedience; it's rest.

Let me be clear: submission is never an excuse for sin or abuse. When earthly commands contradicted God's Word, I learned to obey God rather than men **(Acts 5:29)**—but to do so with the same humility, not contempt. Even in disagreement, a submitted spirit keeps you under God's covering while you stand for righteousness.

Practically, God taught me simple habits that keep pride out and His covering in:

- **Pray before you answer.** Slow down pride; speed up listening **(James 1:19).**

- **Ask for counsel early, not after you've decided.** Seek wisdom, not rubber stamps **(Proverbs 11:14).**

- **Keep short accounts—repent quickly,** forgive quickly, and move on **(Ephesians 4:26–27).**

- **Choose service over spotlight.** Carry a towel before you carry a title **(John 13:14).**

- **Put on Christ daily—consciously** *"dress"* in His character before you walk into conflict **(Romans 13:14).**

Pride left me exposed, but humility kept me protected. When I humbled myself—at home, in ministry, and under leadership—God covered me.

Warfare didn't disappear, but its access points did. *Peace returned. Clarity returned. Favor followed obedience.* And I learned that submission is not losing; it's choosing the winning side—God's order, God's timing, and God's protection.

Love Fulfills the Law

Paul shifts from civic duty to spiritual duty:

"Owe no man any thing, but to love one another: for he that loveth another hath fulfilled the law."

(Romans 13:8)

Laws may regulate behavior, but only love fulfills the heart of God. Commandments against *adultery, murder, theft, and covetousness* are summed up in one principle: love your neighbor as yourself **(v. 9).**

This love is not sentimental but sacrificial. It calls us to treat others with the same dignity, compassion, respect, and patience that Christ shows us.

Walking in the Light

Paul closes with a call to urgency:

"The night is far spent, the day is at hand: let us therefore cast off the works of darkness, and let us put on the armour of light." **(Romans 13:12)**

The Christian Walk is not passive—it is warfare. We must put away *drunkenness, immorality, strife, and envy,* and instead *"put ye on the Lord Jesus Christ"* **(v. 14).** To put on Christ is to live in His character, clothed in His righteousness, and armed with His Spirit.

Reflective Questions:

1. What does it mean for you personally to be "subject to higher powers"?

2. How do you reconcile obeying earthly authority with obeying God's ultimate authority?

3. In what relationships do you need to show love as the fulfillment of the law?

4. What "works of darkness" must you cast off in order to walk more fully in the light?

5. How can putting on Christ daily reshape the way you respond to challenges?

Reflective Summary:

Romans 13 teaches us that faith is practical. It shows in how we respect authority, how we treat our neighbors, and how we live in a world of darkness.

Subjection without love is empty, and love without holiness is shallow. But when we submit to God, walk in love, and clothe ourselves in Christ, we become living witnesses of the gospel.

Prayer

Lord,

Teach us to walk in submission without fear, in love without hypocrisy, and in holiness without compromise.

Help us to honor authority where it does not conflict with Your Word, and give us courage to stand when it does.

Clothe us daily with the armor of light. Let our lives be marked by love, discipline, and obedience, so that the world may see Christ in us.

In Jesus' name, Amen.

Chapter 12 – Liberty, Responsibility, and the Law of Love

After instructing believers about subjection to authority and walking in the light, Paul now turns to life within the church. His message in **Romans 14** is both practical and convicting: we must walk in liberty without wounding others, and live in love without condemning others.

Liberty with Limits

Paul begins:

"Him that is weak in the faith receive ye, but not to doubtful disputations." **(Romans 14:1)**

In other words, welcome the weaker brother, but don't drag him into arguments over minor issues.

Some believers eat everything; others eat only herbs. Some esteem one day above another; others esteem every day alike. The issue is not the food or the day—it is whether each person is honoring the Lord in their conscience.

Christian liberty is not license to do whatever pleases us. It is freedom to honor God without being bound by human traditions, while still walking in patience toward those whose conscience is different from ours.

Responsibility Toward Others

Paul reminds us:

"But why dost thou judge thy brother? or why dost thou set at nought thy brother? for we shall all stand before the judgment seat of Christ."

(Romans 14:10)

Each believer answers to God, not to the opinions of others. Yet liberty is never an excuse to destroy the work of God in someone else's life. If food, drink, or any practice offends or causes a brother to stumble, love calls us to restrain ourselves.

"It is good neither to eat flesh, nor to drink wine, nor any thing whereby thy brother stumbleth, or is offended, or is made weak." **(Romans 14:21)**

Testimony Connection

I believe I have a responsibility to live a model life, to be a good example, and to treat others respectfully, demonstrating my Christian beliefs and values.

My liberty in Christ is real, but it is not about proving what I can do—it is about showing who I belong to. People are watching, and sometimes the only Bible they will read is the life I live before them.

There were times I had to learn this the hard way. In my early walk, I wanted to prove my freedom by doing things that seemed harmless to me, but those choices confused or discouraged others.

I discovered that even if something was permissible, it wasn't always beneficial **(1 Corinthians 10:23).** A careless word, an impatient attitude, or even a habit I excused as *"my liberty"* could become a stumbling block to someone weaker in the faith.

That realization changed how I lived. I began to see that every interaction is a chance to reflect Christ. Every choice is either building someone up or tearing them down.

If my liberty caused another person to stumble, then love called me to lay that liberty down. The Spirit taught me that true strength is not found in demanding my rights but in surrendering them for the sake of another's soul.

So now, I strive to walk with a different mindset. I want *my words to carry peace, my actions to display respect, and my example to point to Christ.* The kingdom of God is not about what I can eat or drink, wear or do—it is about *righteousness, peace, and joy in the Holy Ghost* **(Romans 14:17).**

If my life doesn't lead people toward that reality, then I am missing the heart of my calling.

Living by the Law of Love

Paul concludes:

"Let us therefore follow after the things which make for peace, and things wherewith one may edify another." **(Romans 14:19)**

The measure of our faith is not just how free we are, but how well we love. Love calls us to lay down rights for the sake of another's growth.

Love chooses peace over pride, edification over argument. Liberty without love destroys; liberty with love builds.

Reflective Questions:

1. Where do you struggle with judging others whose convictions differ from yours?

2. How can you use your liberty to serve rather than to stumble others?

3. What is one area where God may be calling you to greater restraint for the sake of unity?

4. How does remembering the "judgment seat of Christ" change the way you treat others?

5. Are your daily choices producing righteousness, peace, and joy in the Holy Ghost?

Reflective Summary:

Romans 14 teaches us that liberty and love must walk hand in hand.

We are free in Christ, but our freedom is never an excuse to wound others. Instead, we are called to live with *patience, humility, and responsibility,* remembering that every believer is Christ's servant and every choice should edify the body.

Prayer:

Lord,

Thank You for the freedom You have given us in Christ. Teach us to walk in that liberty with humility and responsibility.

Help us to build others up instead of tearing them down, to use our freedom for peace and edification, and to remember always that we will give account to You.

Let our lives produce righteousness, peace, and joy in the Holy Ghost.

In Jesus' name, Amen.

Chapter 13 – Unity, Endurance, and Hope

After urging believers in **Romans 14** to walk in liberty without wounding others, Paul now deepens the call in **Romans 15**: *we must carry one another's burdens, pursue unity, and live in hope through the Scriptures.*

Bearing One Another's Burdens

Paul opens:

"We then that are strong ought to bear the infirmities of the weak, and not to please ourselves." **(Romans 15:1)**

Strength is not for self-indulgence but for service. Those who are mature in the faith are called to *carry, not criticize, the weaknesses of others.* Christ Himself is the example:

"For even Christ pleased not himself; but, as it is written, The reproaches of them that reproached thee fell on me." **(Romans 15:3)**

Jesus bore our reproaches, so we must be willing to bear with one another in patience and love.

Endurance Through the Scriptures

Paul then points to the Word of God as our source of endurance and encouragement:

"For whatsoever things were written aforetime were written for our learning, that we through patience and comfort of the scriptures might have hope." **(Romans 15:4)**

The Scriptures remind us that God has always been faithful, and they give us courage to endure. *Without the Word, hope weakens. With the Word, hope anchors us.*

Unity in the Body

Paul's prayer is powerful:

"Now the God of patience and consolation grant you to be likeminded one toward another according to Christ Jesus: That ye may with one mind and one mouth glorify God, even the Father of our Lord Jesus Christ." **(Romans 15:5–6)**

Unity is not sameness—it is harmony. Different voices, backgrounds, and gifts, yet one purpose: *to glorify God.* Division silences worship; unity multiplies it.

Testimony Connection

I have learned in my journey that true strength is not shown in how much I can carry for myself, but in how much I can help carry for others.

There were seasons when I wanted the church to carry me—and they did, thanks to Pastor Gwendolyn McCurry and others who poured into my life when I was weak. Their prayers, counsel, and patience were lifelines that held me together when I could not stand on my own.

But as I grew in Christ under the leader of Pastor James H. Bannerman, I realized I could not remain in that place forever. Just as they carried me, I now had a responsibility to become strong enough to carry someone else.

Maturity meant shifting from being the one always in need to being the one who could meet a need. The same grace that once upheld me was now working through me to uphold others.

I also discovered how vital Scripture is to endurance. There were times in my life when everything around me was unstable— relationships, finances, even my emotions. But when I opened the Word, I found stability that nothing else could give. The Scriptures became my comfort, reminding me that God's promises were bigger than my pain.

Unity has also been a lesson I had to learn the hard way. I have seen how pride and disagreement can tear apart a home, a ministry, or a friendship. But I have also seen how humility and patience restore what seemed broken beyond repair.

Whenever I laid aside my need to be right and sought instead to glorify God, unity followed. And with unity came strength, healing, and a renewed sense of hope.

Hope for the Nations

Paul's vision stretches beyond the Jewish believers to the Gentiles:

"There shall be a root of Jesse, and he that shall rise to reign over the Gentiles; in him shall the Gentiles trust." **(Romans 15:12)**

The hope of the gospel is not limited—it is for all people, all nations, all backgrounds. Paul closes this section with a blessing:

"Now the God of hope fill you with all joy and peace in believing, that ye may abound in hope, through the power of the Holy Ghost." **(Romans 15:13)**

Reflective Questions:

1. How do you respond to the weaknesses of others—by criticism or by carrying?

2. In what areas of your life do you need renewed endurance through the Scriptures?

3. Where do you see division in your relationships, and how might humility restore unity?

4. How does the hope of the gospel challenge you to look beyond your own circle to the nations?

5. Are you living in such a way that others see joy, peace, and hope through the power of the Holy Ghost?

Reflective Summary:

Romans 15 calls us to live beyond ourselves: to carry the weak, to endure through the Scriptures, to walk in unity, and to overflow with hope.

Strength without service is wasted. Knowledge without love is empty. But when we live in humility, anchored in the Word, and filled with the Spirit, our lives become a testimony of Christ's power to a watching world.

Prayer:

Lord,

Make me strong not for myself, but for others. Teach me to carry burdens in love, to endure through Your Word, and to live in unity with my brothers and sisters in Christ.

Fill me with hope through the power of the Holy Ghost, that my life may overflow with joy and peace and point others to You.

In Jesus' name, Amen.

Chapter 14 – Finishing Well with Gratitude and Watchfulness

Romans 16 may look like just a list of names, but it is much more. It shows us Paul's heart as he closes this letter, reminding us that the gospel is not lived in isolation—it is lived in *community, in gratitude, and in faithfulness to the end.*

Honoring Fellow Laborers

Paul greets more than two dozen individuals by name. He honors Priscilla and Aquila, who risked their lives for him. He remembers Mary, who labored much. He acknowledges Andronicus and Junia, fellow prisoners for Christ.

This shows us that no work for the kingdom is forgotten. God values every hand, every prayer, every sacrifice. Ministry is never a one-man show; it is the combined effort of many who give themselves for Christ.

Guarding Against Division

In the midst of his greetings, Paul gives a sharp warning:

"Now I beseech you, brethren, mark them which cause divisions and offences contrary to the doctrine which ye have learned; and avoid them." **(Romans 16:17)**

Division is one of the enemy's oldest tricks. Where unity builds, division destroys. The church must always be watchful, discerning between true servants of Christ and those who use smooth words to deceive.

Testimony Connection

As I reflect on my own journey, I see the importance of both gratitude and watchfulness.

There were many who stood with me when I was weak—mentors, pastors, and friends who labored, prayed, and sacrificed to help me grow.

I thank God for Pastor Gwendolyn McCurry, who poured wisdom and truth into me even when I did not always listen.

I thank God for those in the church who encouraged me when I was discouraged, who covered me in prayer, and who reminded me of God's calling on my life.

At the same time, I also learned to recognize those who caused division—people whose words were smooth but whose motives were not pure.

Early in ministry, I was sometimes too trusting, thinking everyone who said *"Praise the Lord"* was a true servant of Christ. But experience taught me to *discern, to guard my spirit, and to stay rooted in sound doctrine.*

Gratitude keeps you humble; watchfulness keeps you safe.

Glory to God Alone

Paul ends with a doxology:

"To God only wise, be glory through Jesus Christ for ever. Amen." **(Romans 16:27)**

The letter begins with the gospel and ends with glory. Paul never lets the focus drift from Christ. No matter the labor, the sacrifice, or the struggle, the glory always belongs to God alone.

Reflective Questions:

1. Who in your life has labored for your spiritual growth, and how can you honor them?

2. How do you guard yourself and your church against the spirit of division?

3. What role does gratitude play in strengthening your walk with Christ?

4. Where do you need greater discernment between those who build and those who break down?

5. How can you finish your race with the same focus as Paul—giving all glory to God?

Reflective Summary

Romans 16 teaches us that the Christian life is lived in community.

We honor those who labor, guard against those who divide, and give glory to God who sustains us.

Finishing well means living with gratitude and watchfulness until the end.

Prayer:

Father,

Thank You for the people You have placed in my life who labored for my growth and prayed for my soul.

Help me to honor their sacrifices with a life of faithfulness. Give me discernment to recognize division and strength to stand in unity.

And above all, let my life bring glory to You alone, through Jesus Christ my Lord.

Amen.

Epilogue – The Just Shall Live by Faith

From beginning to end, the book of Romans proclaims the heart of the gospel: *"The just shall live by faith."* **(Romans 1:17).**

Paul lays out *the need for salvation, the provision of grace through Jesus Christ, the life of the Spirit, the sovereignty of God, and the call to practical holiness*. Every chapter has shown us that faith is not just an idea—it is a way of life.

Faith justifies. Faith sanctifies. Faith sustains. Faith leads us from darkness into light, from bondage into liberty, from weakness into strength. And this faith is not rooted in ourselves, but in Christ alone.

My own testimony is a witness to this truth. There were seasons of pride, disobedience, and stumbling, but God's grace never let me go.

There were times I ignored wise counsel, made choices that brought pain, or walked in my own way, but the Spirit faithfully drew me back.

The mercy of God restored me, and the Word of God renewed me. What Paul preached, I lived— and what I lived, I now share, that others may learn and walk in faith.

This book has walked us through the full sweep of Romans:

- **Romans 1–3** show us the universal need for salvation.

- **Romans 4–5** reveal the righteousness of God through faith.

- **Romans 6–8** teach us the life of victory in the Spirit.

- **Romans 9–11** remind us of God's sovereignty and faithfulness.

- **Romans 12–15** call us to a practical life of sacrifice, submission, liberty, and unity.

- **Romans 16** closes with gratitude, watchfulness, and glory to God.

Through it all, one message remains unshaken: **the just shall live by faith.**

Final Reflection:

Faith is not a one-time act—it is a daily walk. It is trusting God when the path is clear, and even more when it is not.

It is surrendering pride for humility, liberty for love, and independence for dependence on the Spirit.

Faith makes us not just hearers, but doers. Not just receivers, but givers. Not just survivors, but overcomers.

Closing Exhortation:

As you finish this book, I pray you carry these truths into your own journey. Present your body as a living sacrifice. Walk in the Spirit. Guard against pride. Live in love. Bear with the weak. Strive for unity. And through it all, give glory to God.

The call of Romans is not just to understand the gospel, but to live it. May your life, like Paul's, be a living letter—*written not with ink, but with the Spirit of God, known and read of all men* **(2 Corinthians 3:2–3).**

Final Prayer:

Lord,

We thank You for the gospel revealed in Romans, for the faith that saves, and for the Spirit that sustains.

Teach us to walk by faith, not by sight. Make our lives living sacrifices, our homes houses of peace, and our churches places of unity.

Keep us humble, grateful, and watchful until the day Christ returns. And may all glory be Yours forever.

Amen.

Author's Bio:

Eld Joel Latimore Jr. is a U.S. Army veteran, minister, and author with a heart for teaching God's Word in a way that is both practical and Spirit-led.

Through his own journey of trials, transformation, and testimony, he has learned firsthand the power of faith and the guidance of the Holy Ghost.

He has written multiple books, including *Faith and Fire: Walking with the Holy Ghost and Not This Woman: Delilah's Spirit, the Strange Woman, and the High Price of Disobedience.* His passion is to see believers grow in spiritual maturity, walk in holiness, and experience the fullness of God's calling for their lives.

When he is not writing or ministering, Elder Latimore is engaged in community outreach, mentoring, and encouraging the next generation to live out their faith with boldness.

He continues to inspire others through his writing, preaching, and teaching, always pointing them back to the truth that *"the just shall live by faith."*

Back Cover Blurb:

The Just Shall Live by Faith: Lessons from the book of Romans

The book of Romans is Paul's greatest masterpiece—a Spirit-inspired letter that unveils the righteousness of God and calls believers to a life of faith.

In The Just Shall Live by Faith, Eld Joel Latimore Jr. walks verse by verse through Romans, blending biblical commentary with personal testimony to show how faith transforms both heart and life.

From justification to sanctification, from liberty to love, from unity to endurance, this book will help you:

- Understand the gospel as Paul preached it.

- Learn how to walk in the Spirit and overcome the flesh.

- Embrace liberty without causing others to stumble.

- Live in humility, unity, and hope.

- Apply the truth of Romans to your everyday walk with God.

With reflective questions, summaries, and prayers at the end of each chapter, this devotional commentary is both a study resource and a spiritual companion.

Whether you are new to the faith or seasoned in ministry, this book will remind you that the call of Romans is not just to believe—but to live.

Because truly, *the just shall live by faith.*